THREADS OF A HIDDEN STORY

POEMS OF STRENGTH, SILENCE, AND SURVIVAL

ANSHIKA

Made with ♥ on the Notion Press Platform
www.notionpress.com

For every girl who dared to dream —
even when no one believed in her,
even when the world told her to shrink,
even when love came with conditions.

This is for the ones who weren't protected,
who weren't praised,
who weren't chosen —
but still chose themselves.

You survived.
You are surviving.
You are enough.

Contents

Preface

Threads of a Hidden Story is more than a collection of poems — it is a quiet rebellion, a testimony of survival, and a journey toward self-worth in a world that often silences pain wrapped in silence.

This book began as a whisper — a place to hold the feelings I couldn't speak aloud, the truths too heavy to carry alone. These poems were born from long nights, silent tears, aching questions, and the weight of being seen only in fragments. Writing them was both an unraveling and a rebuilding.

I didn't write these poems to impress, but to express. To survive. To breathe. To make space for the girl who kept smiling through expectations, who kept performing, who kept trying to be enough — even when the world rarely said, "you are."

They are stitched from sleepless nights, unspoken fears, quiet courage, and invisible battles. Each word holds a piece of me — the eldest daughter, the silent fighter, the dreamer who dared to want more even when no one offered permission.

But this is not just my story.

These poems are echoes of so many others — especially the girls who were told to shrink, to wait, to sacrifice, to disappear. If you've ever been made to feel like your voice was too loud or not loud enough, if you've ever questioned your worth because no one else affirmed it — then these pages were written for you too.

Threads of a Hidden Story is a reclaiming. A remembering. A soft, defiant hope.

Thank you for letting these words into your hands, your heart, your story. I hope they remind you that you are not alone, your silence holds power, and your dreams — even the ones you tucked away — are still worth chasing.

This is my truth. And maybe, a part of yours too.

With all my heart,

Anshika

Acknowledgements

To every soul who has ever carried the weight of silence — this book is for
you.
I want to express my deepest gratitude to those who held space for me,
even in my quietest moments.
To the friends who checked in, the family who tried to understand, and
the strangers who found a reflection of themselves in my words —
Thank you.
To the ones who broke me, knowingly or not — your absence taught
me to find strength within myself.
And to the little girl I once was — I'm sorry it took this long to hear
you, to honor you, and to let you speak.
Thank you to every reader who chooses to sit with these poems.
May they offer you comfort, validation, and the reminder that your
story, no matter how hidden, matters.

Prologue

This book holds the voice I was never allowed to use.

Each poem is a piece of my heart that I hid — out of fear, out of duty, out of love that felt more like silence. They were written in the stillness of long nights, between tears no one saw, and dreams I was taught not to chase.

I am the eldest daughter — the quiet fighter, the invisible backbone, the one expected to endure, not to speak.

But these pages are where I finally speak.

They carry the weight of expectations I never asked for, and the ache of becoming everything for everyone but myself. They carry the tenderness of a girl who still dared to dream, even when the world gave her every reason not to.

This isn't just my story.

It's yours too — if you've ever felt unseen.

If you've ever had to be strong when all you wanted was to be held.

If you've ever loved your family deeply, yet lost pieces of yourself trying to be enough for them.

To the girls who were never told they could choose their own path — I see you.

To the women who survived without applause — I believe you.

To the ones who are still learning how to live for themselves — I am with you.

May these words hold your pain gently,

and remind you:

your voice matters.

Your story is sacred.

And even when you feel broken — you are still whole.

Content

Section One

Childhood and Dreams Lost

1. She Dreamed, I Endured

(Begins with childhood hopes and painful transition into adulthood)

The child I used to be would wish the days away,
To grow up fast, to stand and say—
That being a girl won't dim my light,
That I could fight, and I was right.
I dreamed of being what my father sought,
To earn the love that couldn't be bought.
To wear the strength of a son with pride,
To make my parents' dreams collide
With mine, and rise beyond their fears—
That little girl held back her tears.
She hoped, she dreamed, she dared believe,
That love was something she could weave.
And though the stars were out of touch,
She reached for them — she wanted much.
But then… life happened.
The child within me took her bow,
She sleeps in silence somewhere now.
And in her place, an adult stands,
With trembling heart and calloused hands.

Adulthood came with silent screams,
With broken hopes and shattered dreams.
With sleepless nights and thoughts too loud,
With smiles that hide beneath a cloud.
The fairytales were just pretend,
And "happily ever after" had no end.
The warmth of dreams turned into fright,
Expectation became a heavy fight.
Why, they ask, if life is sweet,
Does emptiness still haunt my beat?
Why does hope now make me shake,
And joy feel like a thing I fake?
I regret the wish I made too soon,
To trade my stars for sun and moon.
For all I craved has turned to ache—
A past I'd give the world to take.
Yet somewhere deep, her echo stays,
The child who saw through brighter days.
And maybe, if I still believe,
She'll lend me hope I can retrieve.

2. The Weight Of My Wings

(Yearning for freedom and trust, opening up to pain)

I didn't want a lesson,
I just wanted to be free,
To laugh without a shadow,
To love without a plea.
I opened up too early,
At a time too soft, too young,
Where kindness felt like safety,
And trust rolled off my tongue.
I gave my heart so freely,
Believed in every smile,
But life had other plans for me,
And truth took me a while.

The hands I thought would hold me,
Let go without a sound,
And every time I stumbled,
No one was around.
They called it all a lesson,
As if that makes it fair,
But what I sought was comfort,
A little love, some care.
I didn't want to learn through pain,
Or cry to find my voice,
I only ever wanted
To feel I had a choice.
Now silence is my armor,
And distance is my shield,
But still I dream of feathers,
Unchained and gently healed.
So no—this wasn't wisdom,
It was sorrow in disguise,
But even through the aching,
A softer hope still tries.

3. Whispers Beneath The Silence

(Feeling unheard, lost, and trapped despite others'
reassurances)

They tell me, "Don't lose hope," they say, "Hold on tight,"
That God has a plan, that I'll see the light.
They say my life isn't as hard as it seems,
But they don't hear the silence that buries my dreams.
I wake to a world that feels distant and cold,
Where the stories I wrote are no longer bold.
Where the fire I kindled has flickered and died,
And all that remains is the ache I can't hide.
I gave all I had—my time, my soul,
Chasing their praise, playing their role.
But now I am lost, worn out and small,
A stranger who answers to every call.
My mind forgets that I once knew joy,
That life was more than just a ploy
To make them proud, to win their grace,
While I fade behind a borrowed face.
Surrounded by shadows, I sink in despair,
Caught in a war no one sees, no one shares.

My heart beats quietly, crushed and unheard,
My voice locked away with each unspoken word.
Yet somewhere within, a whisper remains,
Beneath all the sorrow, beneath all the chains.
It calls me back to the dreams I had lost,
To remind me I'm worthy, no matter the cost.
So if you ask me what I miss most—
It's the fire, the freedom, the fearless ghost
Of the soul I once was, the dreams I held tight,
The version of me who still burned with light.

Section Two

<u>The Burden Of Expectations And Emptiness</u>

4. Not Empty Just Hollow

(The ache of invisible pain and emotional emptiness)

They say I only see the dark,
that I chase shadows,
ignore the light.
But how do I explain
I searched for the sun
and came back burned—
tired of trying,
tired of failing
to find something bright in a world
that kept dimming?
They say every fall is a lesson,
every break a blessing in disguise.
Then why do I stand
at the same place I began—
no lesson, no loss,
no gain, no growth—
just the echo of pain
that never quite leaves?
How do I explain
I fear nothing now
because I've already imagined

every worst-case ending—
and mourned them
before they could happen?
They call me an overthinker,
but they don't see
the curse of noticing
the smallest things—
a shift in tone,
an avoided glance,
the silence between the lines.
Deep down,
I am hollow.
Not empty,
but filled with the quiet ache
of knowing that one day,
I will stand alone
with only my suffering
to hold my hand.
I was once
the happy girl,
the hopeful one.
But life,
and they,
taught me otherwise—
taught me that my fears
were never lies,
and my hopes
were only stories
I told myself

ANSHIKA

to sleep at night.

5. Depression With A Smile

(The silent battle of depression masked by smiles)

I chase the end of every day,
Trying to outrun thoughts that stay.
I drain my limbs, I burn my breath,
Hoping sleep will mimic death.
Exhaustion clings like second skin,
But still the war begins within.
Tired eyes, yet wide awake,
Mind a storm I cannot break.
Late night hums with silent screams,
Anxiety kills softer dreams.
Distraction dances, dull and cheap,
Until pain cries itself to sleep.
I wake when morning's nearly done,
A ghost who hides away the sun.
Body begs for rest and peace,
But heartache grants no sweet release.
If this is not depression's face,
Then why this numb and aching place?
A smile stitched in practiced grace,
But hollow in its warmest trace.

I do not beg, I do not plead,
I no longer voice my need.
I let them talk, I let them stare,
Pretend, perhaps, that I don't care.
But deep within, I still rewind,
Still overthink, still stay confined.
The weight of silence, words unsaid,
A heavy heart, a soul half-dead.
So here I breathe, and here I stand,
Not brave, not strong—just barely manned.
But still, I write, and still, I feel,
Hoping words might help me heal.

6. Eldest, But Never Enough

(The poem for the Eldest Daughter)

They say the youngest is loved the most,
The sons are honored, held so close.
But I — the elder, born a girl —
Was cast aside, not given the world.
By birth alone, they marked me wrong,
A burden carried all life long.
Not my fault, this silent weight,
But still, I bend beneath its fate.
I try and try, yet still I'm less,
Good deeds dissolve in thanklessness.
I climb the hills, I break the stone,
But in the end, I stand alone.
They want me gone, to wed, to leave,
To pay a debt I don't believe.
Adjust, obey, don't dream too loud,
Just fade into the silent crowd.
But what of dreams I dare to keep?
What of the tears I cry in sleep?
What of the fire inside my soul,
That's tired of playing every role?

I'm not your shame, your fear, your plan,
I'm not the shadow of a man.
I'm not the debt that must be paid,
Nor broken glass that must be laid.
My pillow knows the truths I hide,
The nights I've wept and hoped and died.
Yet here I breathe, though weak and torn,
Still asking why I had to be born.
Is sleep the end? Is silence peace?
Will this relentless ache just cease?
But something deep inside still pleads,
That maybe love is what I need.
Not duty wrapped in veiled control,
But hands that hold my weathered soul.
Not praise for what I do or give,
But space that lets me choose to live.
So if I fall, please let me land,
Not judged, not scolded — just a hand.
For I am tired, and I am small,
But I have worth, in spite of all.
And maybe, just beyond this night,
There waits a dawn, a softer light.
A life that's mine — no cage, no chain —
Where being me is not in vain.

Section Three

<u>Reflection, Resilience, and Hope</u>

7. Between the Lines of Light

(Life beyond black and white)

We think life's painted black and white,
A path of wrong or shining right.
But hues of grey lie in between,
In places yet to be seen.
The outcome may be loss or gain,
Yet every road won't look the same.
A twist, a turn, a steep incline—
Each step you take still holds a sign.
When dreams fall short, don't lose your flame,
The tunnel's dark, but light still came.
Perhaps you strayed, but not in vain,
Each fall will shape what you attain.
Life is a house of mirrored walls,
You move, you stumble, sometimes fall.
But through the maze, with lessons deep,
You'll find the treasures that you keep.
So fail with pride, and dare to try,
Let questions lift you to the sky.
For coal must bear the fiercest test,
Before it shines among the best.

8. The Line I Drew

(Owning personal effort and bravery, recognizing self-worth)

I stood at the edge of something bright,
Hands full of effort, heart full of night.
The world said "You did it," but I turned away —
"I was lucky," I whispered, "just chance, just play."
The stars aligned, or so I claimed,
As if my sweat had no rightful name.
As if courage was silent, effort unseen,
As if I was just walking someone else's dream.
But there was a fire behind each fear,
A voice that trembled, but still drew near.
A thousand tiny, quiet wars —
And I fought every single one of those wars.
Why then, this weight? This echo inside?
Why do I shrink when I should stride?
Because doubt wears the face of truth sometimes,
And it speaks in the tone of my own old lines.
But now I see it — the line is there,
Between fate and work, between hope and care.
It wasn't the stars that carved my way,
It was me — showing up every day.

So here I stand, not by mistake.
This joy, this peace, this chance I take —
They are not gifts I stole from the sky.
They are seeds I planted, afraid, but spry.
And now they bloom — not luck, not game.
But bravery disguised by another name.
So when life calls me to stand and shine,
I won't step back.
This time, the line is mine.

9. What the Heart Learns Last

(Stages of grief and acceptance)

It starts in hush, a whispered lie,
That all is well, no need to cry.
We close our eyes to cracks that grow,
Afraid to feel, afraid to know.
Then fury comes, a blinding flame,
We look for faces we can blame.
The hurt runs deep, the heart feels weak,
And rage becomes the voice we speak.
We bargain next with trembling hands,
Try to reshape life's shifting sands.
"If only this… if only then,"
We beg to start it all again.
But silence falls, and sorrow stays,
A shadow dulling all our days.
The songs go mute, the colors die,
And joy forgets the way to sky.
At last, a truth begins to rise —
We can't undo, we can't revise.
The harm is done, the past is gone,

It's time to breathe and carry on.
Let go, not to forget the pain,
But free your soul from dragging chains.
Not healing yet, but close, you see —
A step toward peace, a way to be.

10. One of Those Days

(Hold on through tough times)

Life gets hard, and you want to quit,
you wonder if you're made for it.
Maybe this path was never yours,
maybe you're stuck behind closed doors.
You feel like you don't deserve the fight,
like chasing dreams just isn't right.
But pause—
just breathe—
it's not always clear,
you're just caught in a heavy year.
It's just one of those days again,
where strength feels distant, lost in pain.
But maybe this is how you grow,
through phases rough, through depths you know.
Maybe it's how God shapes the clay,
prepares you in His quiet way.
The future once looked soft and sweet,
a fairy tale beneath your feet.
You trusted it would all make sense,
but time can build a different fence.
You used to dream with open skies,

now life just stares with colder eyes.
Back when you were small and free,
you'd long to be who you now see.
To be the boss, to call the shot,
but now you miss what then you got.
The peace, the joy, the slower pace,
the warmth of home, the open space.
You didn't know how soft it was—
and now it's gone, without applause.
But hear this now—don't walk away,
don't throw your worth to one hard day.
You're not incapable, just tired,
not lost, not broken, not expired.
Live for the dreams you used to chase,
for younger you, that hopeful face.
They knew you'd fall but still believed,
that every wound would be redeemed.
So hold on tight, you've come so far,
you're braver than you think you are.
This isn't failure, this is grace.
It's just one of those days.
Just one tough place.

Quiet Exit

If you've made it to this page, thank you — not just for reading, but for feeling.

This book began as a quiet place to put the parts of myself I was too afraid to say out loud. It became a mirror, a map, a form of healing. I never expected anyone else to walk these words with me — and yet, here you are.

I hope something within these lines helped you feel seen. I hope you carry away not just the weight of what hurts, but the strength of what survives.

You are not your pain.

You are not your silence.

You are still becoming.

And that becoming is beautiful.

So take a deep breath.

You made it.

And you are not alone.

With love and light,

Anshika